THE TOWER OF LONDON AS IT WAS

by

G. ABBOTT

Yeoman Warder (Retd)
H.M. Tower of London

THE TOWER OF LONDON.

Front cover: The Tower, from the Thames. From an engraving after E. Duncan
Inside front cover: Map of The Tower 1597

Published by Hendon Publishing Co. Ltd., Hendon Mill, Nelson, Lancashire
Text © G. Abbott, 1988
Printed by Fretwell & Cox Ltd., Goulbourne St., Keighley, West Yorkshire BD21 1PZ.

Introduction

Built in 1078 on the orders of William the Conqueror, Her Majesty's Royal Palace and Fortress, the Tower of London, is one of the oldest buildings in the world. After its completion, a further four hundred years would pass before the construction of the Vatican and the Kremlin, five hundred years before the discovery of Canada and seven centuries before the independence of the American colonies. The Tower, a royal residence for nearly six hundred years, has in its time been a royal court, a state prison, Mint, jewel house, observatory, armoury and zoo.

During the life of any building changes take place, depending on the needs of the occupants. Even a castle as 'permanent' as the Tower of London has served so many different purposes over the centuries that more buildings have had to be added, others altered, extended or even demolished when no longer required. Disasters such as fire and bombing have also taken their toll, whilst restoration and repair involves minor alterations.

The pictures in this book, most of them from the author's extensive collection of postcards of the Tower, reveal some of the many changes which have taken place in and around the castle. Having lived in the Tower for eight years, Yeoman Warder Abbott is well qualified to present this pictorial record and so bring back scenes of the Tower as it appeared to past generations of visitors.

This book is dedicated to the memory of Yeoman Warder Samuel Reeves, killed when his home in the North Bastion was destroyed by bombs on 5 October 1940.

It is generally believed that the only changes to the Tower of London were as a result of bomb damage during the Second World War. This is partially true, for the North Bastion (extreme left, jutting from the outer wall) received direct hits and was never rebuilt. Other buildings also sustained severe damage but fortunately the more ancient towers survived intact. During the last one hundred years many other structural and social changes have taken place, as the following pages show.

The Tower has always attracted tourists, but hansom cabs no longer line the approach roads. Instead coaches and cars bring visitors from every country in the world. The viewing public were first admitted in the days of Charles II, mainly to see the Crown Jewels, and so provided Colonel Blood with the opportunity to steal the precious Regalia in 1671. Although the card is dated New Year's Day 1902, it will be noticed that Tower Bridge, completed in 1894, is still under construction.

A Victorian artist's impression of the Middle Tower at the castle's entrance. Only the building itself and the uniform of the yeoman warders are unchanged; the top hats and frock coats, bustles and skirts have been replaced by modern T-shirts and jeans. The white-topped bollards — actually cannon captured from the French during the Napoleonic Wars — were dug out and discarded decades ago, even the one which served as the base of a useful gas lamp.

Built about 1235, the Tower Menagerie was situated just outside the Middle Tower and originally housed wild beasts presented to the monarch by foreign royalty. The animals in its semi-circular enclosures and galleries (above, in 1820) were great attractions for the Londoners but its position at the castle's entrance proved so obstructive that in 1834 the animals were moved, to form the London Zoo in Regents Park, and by 1850 the Menagerie buildings had been completely demolished.

The By-Ward Tower.

Until 1843 the Tower of London was truly a moated castle, though the arch visible on the left had replaced an earlier drawbridge. Behind the boat can be seen the private entrance for royal visitors, its foot-bridge and iron operating wheel still being in position today, but the guardroom to the right has long since been swept away, leaving the Wharf clear of buildings.

Yeoman Warders, guardians of the Tower for over nine centuries, are also members of the Sovereign's Bodyguard of the Yeomen of the Guard Extraordinary. They and their families live in the Tower, and for normal duties the yeoman warders wear the undress uniform seen on the right. For royal visits and similar State occasions they wear State Dress of scarlet and gold, with ruff, sword and partizan. Today's yeoman warders bear the letters 'ER' (Elizabeth Regina) on their uniforms, but those pictured above in 1907 served Edward Rex, and wear medals won in the Boer War and Sudan campaigns.

Here elegant Victorian ladies and their companions study Traitors' Gate, beneath whose arch passed the boats which brought Anne Boleyn and Katherine Howard, Sir Thomas More, Sir Walter Raleigh and scores of others to prison and subsequent execution. This entrance, dry for many years, has recently been refilled in order to present a more authentic appearance.

Traitors' Gate, as seen from the Wharf in 1896, still had the thick sidewalls built earlier that century to prevent influx of water if the moat was flooded. The aspect was improved when the walls were eventually demolished, though there seems little prospect of the gates also being removed and replaced by a portcullis, the original barrier to the Gate. The grooves which guided the portcullis are still visible, though the winch mechanism above the Gate has long since been dismantled.

Near the Middle Drawbridge where now is situated the recently completed History Gallery, the above gun carriage attracted the tourists in the days before the First World War. The engraved brass plate states that it was used to convey Queen Victoria's coffin in the funeral procession at Windsor in 1901, and used again for the same purpose nine years later following the death of King Edward VII.

Ninety years ago the Bloody Tower arch presented a scene of peaceful tranquillity. The rickety sign 'To the Regalia' directed the few visitors to the Crown Jewels, at that time housed in the Wakefield Tower on the right of our picture, and the yeoman warder could rest undisturbed. Now the Main Guard building, seen through the archway, and the warder's box have long since gone, and the Jewels glitter elsewhere.

From the other, north, side of the Bloody Tower arch can be seen the nineteenth-century entrance to the Jewel Chamber, leading via spiral stairs into the Wakefield Tower where the Regalia was displayed. The entrance hall, together with the adjoining building on the left, were destroyed by enemy action in 1941.

The Crown Jewels have been held in the Tower of London since the thirteenth century, in various locations. In 1869 they were housed in the Wakefield Tower, in the room seen above, traditionally believed to be that in which Henry VI was murdered in 1471. But as the numbers of visitors steadily increased after the Second World War, the confined area of the chamber made viewing totally inadequate and in 1967 a new Jewel House was constructed in the Waterloo Block, their present location.

In 1858 an 'undress' uniform was introduced, to be worn on normal daily duty in place of the scarlet and gold State Dress. The black velvet Tudor bonnet of the State Dress continued to be worn, however, as shown by the above yeoman warder leaning against the door of the Bloody Tower. This continued to be the regulation wear until 1885, when an 'undress' hat was designed to match the new uniform. Of similar shape to the Tudor bonnet, it was and is of dark blue cloth with a red and blue cockade at the front, and a red ribbon around the base of the crown. These changes to the 'Beefeaters' uniforms were strongly deplored by indignant letter writers to the London newspapers of August 1885.

Today's visitors will find an upper and a lower room in the Bloody Tower, unlike the one large room shown in the early picture above. Originally a floor was inserted in 1603 for Sir Walter Raleigh's imprisonment, but some time after his execution by the axe in 1618 the floor was removed, a new one being constructed after the Second World War.

Making the most of the Bloody Tower's evil reputation, prefabricated 'ghosts' such as these catered to the public's imagination earlier this century. But such supernatural occurrences should not be discounted altogether, for eerie sightings have been reported in recent years, even by unsuspecting tourists. Now if they had had *their* cameras ready . . . . ?!

Victorian visitors linger on Tower Green, whilst in the foreground the duty Guards NCO ensures that the bugler sounds the correct call. Beyond the heavy artillery piece the area surrounding the execution site is cobbled, whereas nowadays lawns enhance the surrounds of the Beauchamp Tower (left) and the Chapel Royal.

A police constable stands on duty in this 1905 picture, in the days when three inspectors and twenty constables maintained order in the Tower. Since about 1922, however, the yeoman warders took over their duties, with full powers of arrest. Early orders stated that 'should a civilian doubt that the Warder is also a Constable, then the official police baton held in the Ticket Office should be produced as Authority'!

Visitors to the Chapel Royal of St Peter ad Vincula will note the differences between its appearance in the 1880s and today. Gone are the oak pews and pulpit, the reredos and the old-fashioned lighting. Even the alabaster tomb, left of picture, which was made for Sir Richard Cholmondeley and his wife in 1522, was moved to another corner of the chapel in the latest modernisation, its completion being celebrated by HM Queen Elizabeth at a Service of Thanksgiving on 27 May 1971.

Half a century ago and more, the Broadwalk in front of the White Tower was the parade ground for the soldiers of the garrison, and members of the public were kept away from its cobbled area by the long steel barriers seen in the illustration. Ancient cannon were displayed in the Gun Park, and the White Tower's round turret was enhanced by four clock faces in its circular apertures. On the extreme right can be seen the Main Guard, the military headquarters bombed in the Second World War.

North-East View of the White Tower.

The annex along the left side of the White Tower, seen here in 1820, was built in the fourteenth century and formed part of the Queen's Lodgings when royalty lived in the Tower of London. It was later used as offices but was demolished by 1885. The small building at the right-hand end of the White Tower was a guardroom until 1841 when it too was demolished. Removal of these buildings restored the White Tower to its original solitary splendour as seen today.

South-East View of the White Tower, and of the New Horse Armoury.

The single storey annex seen left, was built about 1826 to house effigies of mounted monarchs, but was demolished in 1883. It stood on the site of the medieval Jewel House and other buildings which, when demolished in July 1674, revealed a buried chest containing the remains of two small boys. They were presumed to be those of the two little Princes believed murdered in 1483, and were re-interred with honour in Westminster Abbey.

Here, pictured in 1836, is the interior of the New Horse Armoury. The 'Line of Kings', representing the monarchs in their own armour, was first assembled in the seventeenth century and was moved into this building in 1825, when it was rearranged to correct the wild discrepancies among the exhibits, such as William the Conqueror carrying a musket! When the building was demolished in 1883 the figures were moved within the White Tower, where they are still on display.

Arms and equipment for 100,000 men were once stored ready for use within the Tower of London, many weapons being manufactured in its foundries and workshops. Now the White Tower contains the Royal Armouries, one of the finest collections in the world. But no longer do the knights stand as if on parade at Crécy or Agincourt. Instead glass cases shield them from theft and corrosion, and so unavoidably destroy the illusion.

The Order of the Bath originated in the Chapel Royal of St John the Evangelist within the White Tower, in 1399. Here the knights-to-be knelt in vigil, their armour around the altar. Later, whilst bathing themselves, the king would make the sign of the cross on their backs. When dressed, they were knighted by the monarch and, wearing the robes of the Order, then accompanied the king in his coronation procession to Westminster Abbey.

This is the underground cavern beneath the White Tower, believed to have been the medieval torture chamber, and during the nineteenth century the discovery was reported of the holes in which the supports of the rack had once stood! In our Victorian picture the stone walls and earthen floor recall the chamber's grisly past, but today's visitors walk on wooden floors, whilst the trophies and exhibits adorning the walls are illuminated by modern lighting, leaving little to the imagination.

The imposing building facing the White Tower is the Grand Storehouse. Built in 1689, 370 feet long, it housed arms for 60,000 men and many trophies of war, but on 30 October 1841 it was burnt to the ground, the intense heat melting the lead pipes on the White Tower opposite, and its stocks of gunpowder had to be dumped in the moat for safety. For nine hours the fire raged, and little survived among the charred ruins. On its site was built the Waterloo Block, which now houses the Jewel House.

The devastating fire which, on 30 October 1841, totally destroyed the Grand Storehouse and all its military stores, also spread to the nearby Martin Tower which at that time was the Jewel House. Yeoman Warders and police fought their way in and despite the intense heat and burning timbers, managed to force open the display cases and extract the many crowns, sceptres and other priceless items of the Regalia. Thanks to their heroic efforts not one piece of the nation's treasure was lost or damaged.

From the thirteenth century the safest place in which to convert gold and silver into the nation's coinage was the Tower. Above is the Coining Press Room in the eighteenth century, where boys swung the weighted arms round, applying the pressure needed to stamp the designs on the gold blanks. But despite the inventive genius of Sir Isaac Newton, Master of the Mint 1699–1727, modernisation was eventually necessary, and the Mint moved out of the Tower in 1812.

This 1930s picture of schoolgirls in neat blazers and regulation hats leaving the Middle Drawbridge contrasts sharply with today's crowds of students in their T-shirts and jeans. In those distant days too, a guardsman stood on sentry duty on the Wharf, admired by all who passed by. But the deterioration in public manners, the lack of respect shown by society, has resulted in the removal of both sentry and box to a less approachable area within the castle itself.

Edwardian gentlemen in top hats and frock coats, their ladies in ankle length dresses and straw boaters, stroll leisurely along the Tower Wharf, across the cobbles where now the thousands of sparsely clad runners in the annual London Marathon race past the kiosks and litter bins.

For hundreds of years the Tower's guns positioned along the Wharf have fired to announce great events and royal occasions. The type of artillery varied depending on the armament of the day, that above being the carronades and chamber guns of 1847. Nowadays the Honourable Artillery Company perform the duty, utilising four field guns which, being capable of rapid reloading, reduces the number of guns required.

Within the castle, the long flat-roofed building to the left of the White Tower was the Main Guard, built in 1841, demolished and replaced by a Victorian style building in 1899. On the right of the picture, Tower Bridge, completed in 1894, is seen still under construction. Scaffolding surrounds its foundations, timber litters the beach, and its approach road is still being built.

The official opening by HRH The Prince of Wales on 30 June 1894 was a great day for Londoners. Boats large and small were packed with excited spectators, ships bedecked with flags and bunting, and bands played a fanfare as the Prince operated the controls to raise the mighty bascules. Then, together with the Princess of Wales and the Duke of York, he boarded the steam yacht *Palm* and led a parade of river craft beneath the new bridge *en route* to Westminster Pier.

The royal cavalcade passing the Tower of London after the official opening of Tower Bridge on 30 June 1894. Paddle-steamers, pleasure craft and rowing boats jostled for the best viewing positions, whilst on shore every wall and battlement was packed with spectators. Dignitaries of the Tower and the City lined the Tower Wharf, the scene being made even more splendid by the Life Guards whose burnished helmets and breastplates are visible on the left of the picture.

Things are not always what they seem! This Edwardian postcard apparently shows the King and Queen being rowed in the Royal Barge past the crowds on Tower Wharf. However, close inspection reveals that the royal couple are just two dimensional cut-outs, and the spectators were painted in. But the barge, built of oak in 1689 for William III to travel between the palaces at Windsor and Greenwich, is genuine — as is the Tower of London!

For more than nine centuries warships have moored by the Tower, the nearest anchorage to the heart of the City. Here naval cruisers are on station during the First World War for defence and replenishment. Nowadays modern warships of NATO and other forces visit the Pool of London and their captains continue the ancient tradition of forthwith coming to the Tower of London, there to assure the Resident Governor of their peaceful intentions towards the City.

The view from Tower Bridge in 1906 shows on the right the deserted Tower Wharf. Tower pier has yet to be built, and a paddle-steamer sails past the cargo barges moored near fishing boats off-loading at Billingsgate market. But eighty years later, diesels have replaced paddles, and cargoes go to Rotterdam. Billingsgate has moved away, and the Wharf is thronged with tourists from every corner of the globe.

The old London Bridge once adorned by the heads of traitors executed in the nearby Tower of London, was eventually replaced in 1831 by the one seen above. But this too was dismantled in turn, and in 1967 was rebuilt, spanning a lake in Arizona, USA. No horse omnibuses rumble across the latest London Bridge, no paddle-steamers pass through its arches, and the once steepled skyline is disfigured by soaring office buildings and high-rise blocks of flats.

Just as the Tower protected London, so the nearby Customs House levied taxes on foreign goods brought to the City. The first Customs House on this site was built in 1385, a later one of 1753 being shown above. Here ships' captains would report to declare their cargoes and pay their dues, and although this magnificent building was destroyed by fire in 1814, its modern successor still performs the same function of levying customs and excise for the nation's financial benefit.

Adjoining the Tower of London is St Katherine's Dock, shown above in the 1870s. It was built in 1828, requiring the demolition of 1250 houses and tenements. Scores of ships could berth here, cargoes of tea, brandy, spices, silks, cotton and other goods being hoisted into the warehouses by cranes operated by 16-foot diameter treadwheels turned by eight men pacing inside them. But modernisation took its toll and now the Tower's turrets look down on to hotels and a yacht marina.

On 9 April 1747 Tower Hill was packed with spectators gathered to watch the execution of Simon, Lord Lovat, Jacobite rebel leader. Mounted troops held the crowds back, roof tops were packed and (centre right) a collapsing stand killed many people. Lovat, supported by yeoman warders, died bravely, the last man to be executed by the axe in this country.

Site of Ancient Scaffold.
Here the Earl of Kilmarnock & Lord Balmerino
suffered 18ᵀᴴ August. 1746. Many others were executed here. Trinity S? Gardens. E.C

When the above picture was taken in 1913, the site of the public executions on Tower Hill was in a secluded little park surrounded by trees. Now an impressive war memorial to the Merchant Navy of both World Wars dominates the area, and towering office blocks and the Underground station have replaced the trees and banished the solitude.

Overlooking the public execution site on Tower Hill where so many of the Tower's prisoners were beheaded, stands All Hallows Church, seen above in 1750. It was founded in AD 675 and originally belonged to the Abbey of Barking, in Essex. In 1666 Samuel Pepys viewed the Great Fire from its steeple, and the church itself suffered catastrophic bomb damage in the Second World War. Now restored to its former glory, it is one of the City's leading churches and contains many priceless relics.

Only yards from the Tower's gates a small kiosk-like building leads down to what was London's first underground railway! Built in 1869, a cable operated carriage on a 2′6″ gauge railway took passengers under the river to the opposite bank, a journey made more alarming by the thudding of the paddle-steamers overhead! The completion of Tower Bridge in 1894 led to the closure of the Tower Subway, and it is now used as a conduit for cables and pipelines.

The Royal Mint, built in 1810, stood just north-east of the Tower moat and housed steam driven machinery to improve coin production. But in the late 1960s the Mint moved to Wales, and these impressive buildings are now scheduled for redevelopment. The cobbles and carts of Royal Mint Street, earlier known as Rosemary Lane where once lived Richard Brandon, executioner of Charles I, have long since given way to tarmac, trucks and traffic lights.

For six centuries the moat was the outermost defence until, in 1843, its stagnant waters were drained, revealing ancient cannon balls and stone shot, bones, bottles and similar artifacts. Its depths were then filled in with tons of oyster shells, oysters being cheap and plentiful in those days, and finally turfed over. Since then the moat has been used as a parade ground, a recreation area, and even as a barrage balloon site as part of London's defences during the Second World War.